YOUR PERSONAL MANUAL FOR LIVING YOUR BEST LIFE

A 40-DAY JOURNEY TOWARD HAPPINESS AND ORGANIZATION

CLAUDIO ALVAREZ

Your Personal Manual for Living Your Best Life

Author: Claudio Alvarez

ISBN: 979-8-9912197-8-5

First edition, 2026

*To all those who strive for growth, clarity, and purpose—
may this manual be your companion on the journey
toward your highest self, guiding you one reflection, one
intention, and one step at a time.*

— Claudio Alvarez

Dear reader,

This manual is born from a profound conviction: we all have within us the capacity to create a life with clarity, purpose, and fulfillment. For years, I searched for tools that would help me organize my thoughts, goals, and actions. I discovered that the most valuable thing is having a guide that you can build and evolve yourself with.

"Your personal manual for living your best life" is not a book to read and put on a shelf; it's a travel companion. You'll find reflections, questions, and activities that invite you to look inward, plan with intention, and take concrete steps toward the life you've always dreamed of.

My wish is that each page becomes a mirror of your progress and a reminder of your greatness. It doesn't matter where you are on your journey: you can always begin again, adjust your course, and move forward.

Thank you for taking this step. May this manual serve you as both a beacon and a map on your journey toward your best self.

With appreciation,
Claudio Alvarez

PREFACE

This is your guided space for designing a life with clarity, purpose, and growth.

This manual has been created in two editions: one in Spanish and one in English. The purpose is to make this journey accessible to a wider audience while staying true to its original inspiration.

Both versions contain the same structure, prompts, and motivational quotes, so you can follow the 40-day journey in the language you feel most comfortable with.

Whether you are reading this in Spanish or English, my wish is the same, that this manual helps guide you toward clarity, purpose, and your best self.

— Claudio Alvarez

INTRODUCTION

This manual is your guide, not a set of rigid rules. It's a tool for your personal growth: a space to explore, reflect, and build the life you desire. Over the next 40 days, I invite you to write, dream, and plan.

Turn this book into the blueprint for your best life.

Congratulations on starting this journey!

How to Use This Manual

This manual is designed as a guided journal to help you reflect, grow, and take intentional steps each day.

Here are a few simple suggestions to get the most out of your 40-day journey:

1. One Day at a Time

Focus on just one day's prompt at a time. There is no rush—what matters is your honesty and consistency.

2. Create a Space for Reflection

Find a quiet place where you can write without distractions. Allow yourself 10–20 minutes daily.

3. Be Honest with Yourself

These pages are for you. Write openly and truthfully, without judgment.

4. Revisit Your Answers

At the end of the 40 days, look back at your reflections. Notice how your thoughts, values, and goals may have shifted.

5. Use the Lines for Journaling

Each prompt includes lined pages so you can write freely, just like in a personal journal.

This is your journey—move at your own pace, and let the process guide you.

PHASE 1: ESTABLISHING THE FOUNDATIONS OF YOUR LIFE

(DAYS 1-10)

DAY 1: INTRODUCE YOUR LIFE MANUAL CONCEPT

Concept: A life manual is your personal guide. It's a document that contains everything important to you, from your purpose to your goals. It's the blueprint for living your best life.

Activity: Reflect on the idea of having a comprehensive guide for your life. Consider how a driver's manual helps you drive, or how the Bible serves as a spiritual guide; your manual will be your personal guide for achieving your best life.

Write here:

WHAT DOES THE IDEA OF HAVING A PERSONAL GUIDE FOR YOUR LIFE MEAN TO YOU? WHAT DO YOU HOPE IT HELPS YOU ACHIEVE?

_____

_____

_____

_____

DAY 2: REFLECT ON THE NEED FOR A LIFE GUIDE

Concept: Often, important life lessons and long-term goals get neglected due to daily priorities. You need a tool to help you remember your long-term objectives and live each day to the fullest.

Activity: Think about times when you've felt direction-less or when important lessons have been forgotten.

Write here:

IN WHAT MOMENTS HAVE YOU FELT ADRIFT? WHAT IMPORTANT LIFE LESSONS HAVE YOU FORGOTTEN OVER TIME?

_____

_____

_____

_____

_____

DAY 3: DECIDE ON YOUR MANUAL'S FORMAT

Concept: Choose between a digital format (Excel, MS Word, Evernote) or a physical format (a notebook). Digital offers ease of editing and access; physical allows you the tactile experience of writing.

Activity: Research format options. Try creating a sample page in both digital and physical formats.

Write here:

WHAT FORMAT DO YOU CHOOSE FOR YOUR MANUAL AND WHY?

_____

_____

_____

_____

ADVANTAGES OF THE CHOSEN FORMAT:

_____

_____

_____

_____

_____

_____

DAY 4: DISCOVER YOUR LIFE PURPOSE

Concept: Your manual should include your life purpose. This is one of the central sections and requires deep thought and reflection.

Activity: Dedicate time to reflect. Ask yourself: "Why am I here? What do I want to accomplish with my life?" Write drafts of your life purpose. It doesn't have to be perfect: it's a work in progress.

Write here:

MY LIFE PURPOSE DRAFTS.

DRAFT 1:

_____

_____

_____

_____

_____

DRAFT 2:

_____

_____

_____

DRAFT 3:

_____

_____

_____

_____

_____

_____

_____

DAY 5: IDENTIFY YOUR CORE VALUES

Concept: Values are the principles that guide your decisions and actions.

Activity: List 5-10 key values that are most important to you.

Write here:

Value 1: _____

WHY IS IT IMPORTANT?

_____

_____

_____

_____

_____

Value 2: _____

WHY IS IT IMPORTANT?

_____

_____

_____

_____

_____

Value 3: _____

WHY IS IT IMPORTANT?

_____

_____

_____

_____

_____

Value 4: _____

WHY IS IT IMPORTANT?

_____

_____

_____

_____

_____

Value 5: _____

WHY IS IT IMPORTANT?

_____

_____

_____

_____

_____

DAY 6: RECOGNIZE YOUR STRENGTHS AND AREAS FOR IMPROVEMENT

Concept: Knowing your strengths and weaknesses is essential for personal growth.

Activity: Make a list of 5 strengths and 5 areas for improvement. Consider how you can leverage your strengths to address areas for improvement.

MY 5 STRENGTHS:

_____

_____

_____

_____

_____

MY 5 AREAS FOR IMPROVEMENT:

_____

_____

_____

_____

_____

HOW CAN I UTILIZE MY STRENGTHS TO ENHANCE MY WEAKER AREAS?

_____

_____

_____

_____

_____

_____

DAY 7: CREATE YOUR PERSONAL MOTTOS

Concept: These are your personal mottos for living a great life; they can be inspiring quotes or phrases of your own.

Activity: Collect 3-5 quotes or create your own mottos that inspire you. Write them in your manual.

The best is yet to come.

MY PERSONAL MOTTOS:

_____

_____

_____

_____

_____

_____

DAY 8: DEFINE YOUR IDEAL LIFE VISION

Having a clear vision of how you want your life to be helps you make decisions that align with your goals.

Activity: Imagine your ideal life in 10 years. Describe in detail how you see yourself, what you're doing, where you live, and with whom you share your life.

MY IDEAL LIFE VISION:

_____

_____

_____

_____

_____

_____

IN MY PERSONAL LIFE:

_____

_____

_____

_____

_____

_____

IN MY CAREER/WORK:

_____

_____

_____

_____

_____

_____

IN MY RELATIONSHIPS:

_____

_____

_____

_____

_____

_____

IN MY HEALTH AND WELLBEING:

_____

_____

_____

_____

_____

_____

_____

DAY 9: IDENTIFY YOUR LIFE ROLES

Concept: We all have multiple roles (parent, professional, friend, etc.). Recognizing them helps you better balance your time and energy.

Activity: List your primary roles and define what success means in each one.

MY LIFE ROLES:

Role 1: _____

WHAT DOES SUCCESS MEAN IN THIS ROLE?

_____

_____

_____

_____

_____

Role 2: _____

WHAT DOES SUCCESS MEAN IN THIS ROLE?

_____

_____

_____

_____

_____

_____

_____

Role 3: _____

WHAT DOES SUCCESS MEAN IN THIS ROLE?

_____

_____

_____

_____

_____

_____

_____

Role 4: _____

WHAT DOES SUCCESS MEAN IN THIS ROLE?

_____

_____

_____

_____

_____

Role 5: _____

WHAT DOES SUCCESS MEAN IN THIS ROLE?

_____

_____

_____

_____

_____

DAY 10: ESTABLISH YOUR PERSONAL MISSION

Concept: Your personal mission summarizes how you plan to live and contribute to the world, based on your values and purpose.

Activity: With everything you've discovered, draft your personal mission statement.

MY PERSONAL MISSION STATEMENT:

_____

_____

_____

_____

_____

HOW WILL I LIVE ACCORDING TO THIS MISSION DAILY?

_____

_____

_____

_____

_____

_____

PHASE 2: DETAILED PLANNING AND ACTION

(DAYS 11-20)

DAY 11: BREAK DOWN YOUR LONG-TERM GOALS

Concept: Break down your life goals into smaller objectives: 5-year, 3-year, and 1-year plans.

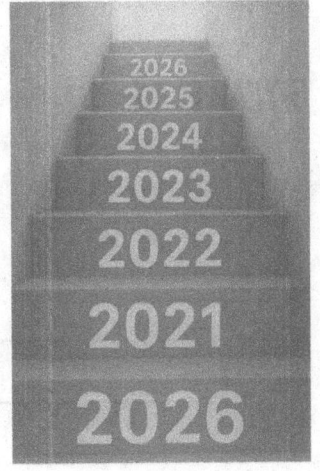

Activity: For your primary goal, write what you need to accomplish in the next 5, 3, and 1 year.

MAIN LIFE GOAL:

_____
_____
_____
_____
_____
_____

5-YEAR PLAN:

_____
_____
_____
_____
_____

3-YEAR PLAN:

_____

_____

_____

_____

_____

_____

1-YEAR PLAN:

_____

_____

_____

_____

_____

_____

DAY 12: SET SHORT-TERM GOALS

Concept: Break down your 1-year goal into quarterly, monthly, and weekly objectives.

Activity: Identify specific milestones or tasks by quarter, month, and week.

1-YEAR GOAL:

_____

_____

_____

_____

_____

Objectives by quarter:

Q1 (JANUARY-MARCH):

_____

_____

_____

_____

_____

_____

Q2 (APRIL-JUNE):

_____

_____

_____

_____

_____

_____

_____

Q3 (JULY-SEPTEMBER):

_____

_____

_____

_____

_____

_____

_____

Q4 (OCTOBER-DECEMBER):

_____

_____

_____

_____

_____

_____

_____

MONTHLY GOALS FOR THE NEXT MONTH:

_____

_____

_____

_____

_____

_____

WEEKLY GOALS FOR THE NEXT WEEK:

_____

_____

_____

_____

_____

_____

_____

DAY 13: DESIGN ACTION PLANS AND MILESTONES

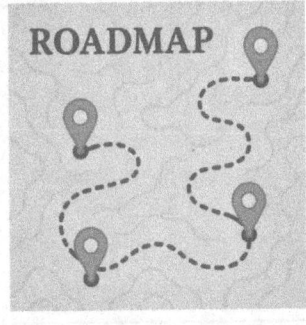

Concept: Develop detailed action plans and establish intermediate milestones to track and celebrate progress.

Activity: For a short-term goal, create a step-by-step plan and identify 2-3 milestones.

SELECTED GOAL:

_____

_____

_____

_____

_____

_____

Action plan (specific steps):

STEP 1:

_____

_____

_____

_____

_____

_____

STEP 2:

_____

_____

_____

_____

_____

_____

_____

STEP 3:

_____

_____

_____

_____

_____

_____

_____

STEP 4:

_____

_____

_____

_____

_____

_____

_____

STEP 5:

_____

_____

_____

_____

_____

_____

_____

MILESTONES TO CELEBRATE:

Milestone 1: _____

Date: _____

Milestone 2: _____

Date: _____

Milestone 3: _____

Date: _____

DAY 14: PLAN FOR OBSTACLES IN ADVANCE

Concept: Anticipate potential obstacles and plan how you'll handle them.

Activity: Review your calendar for the next month. Are there events or busy periods that could interfere with your goals?

Potential obstacles:

OBSTACLE 1:

_____

_____

_____

_____

_____

PLAN TO OVERCOME IT:

_____

_____

_____

_____

_____

OBSTACLE 2:

_____

_____

_____

_____

_____

_____

_____

PLAN TO OVERCOME IT:

_____

_____

_____

_____

_____

_____

OBSTACLE 3:

_____

_____

_____

_____

_____

_____

_____

PLAN TO OVERCOME IT:

_____

_____

_____

_____

_____

_____

GENERAL STRATEGIES TO STAY ON TRACK:

_____

_____

_____

_____

_____

_____

_____

DAY 15: CONNECT YOUR GOALS WITH DAILY HABITS

Concept: Habits aligned with your goals make progress easier.

Activity: Identify 1-3 daily habits that will help you reach a key goal.

SELECTED GOAL:

_____

_____

_____

_____

_____

_____

HABIT 1:

_____

_____

_____

_____

_____

WHEN WILL I DO IT?

_____

_____

_____

_____

_____

_____

_____

HOW WILL I ENSURE THAT I DO IT?

_____

_____

_____

_____

_____

_____

_____

HABIT 2:

_____

_____

_____

_____

_____

_____

_____

WHEN WILL I DO IT?

_____

_____

_____

_____

_____

_____

_____

HOW WILL I MAKE SURE TO DO IT?

_____

_____

_____

_____

_____

_____

HABIT 3:

_____

_____

_____

_____

_____

_____

WHEN WILL I DO IT?

_____

_____

_____

_____

_____

_____

_____

HOW WILL I ENSURE THAT I DO IT?

_____

_____

_____

_____

_____

_____

_____

DAY 16: CREATE YOUR TRACKING SYSTEM

Concept: What gets measured gets improved. You need a system to track your progress.

Activity: Design a simple system to record your goals and habits.

How will I track my goals?

- ☐ Journal/Diary
- ☐ Mobile app
- ☐ Spreadsheet
- ☐ Calendar
- ☐ Other:

Metrics I will measure:

FOR MY MAIN GOAL:

_____

_____

_____

_____

_____

_____

FOR MY DAILY HABITS:

_____

_____

_____

_____

_____

_____

HOW OFTEN WILL I REVIEW MY PROGRESS?

☐ Daily
☐ Weekly
☐ Monthly

WHAT WILL I DO IF I'M NOT PROGRESSING AS EXPECTED?

_____

_____

_____

_____

_____

_____

_____

DAY 17: IDENTIFY YOUR RESOURCES AND TOOLS

Concept: To reach your goals, you'll need resources: time, money, knowledge, connections, and tools.

Activity: List the resources you need and how you'll obtain them.

For my main goal, I need:

TIME: WHERE WILL I FIND THIS TIME?

_____

_____

_____

_____

_____

_____

_____

MONEY/BUDGET:

_____

_____

_____

_____

_____

_____

_____

HOW WILL I OBTAIN IT?

_____

_____

_____

_____

_____

_____

KNOWLEDGE/SKILLS:

_____

_____

_____

_____

_____

_____

HOW WILL I ACQUIRE THEM?

_____

_____

_____

_____

_____

_____

_____

CONNECTIONS/NETWORK:

_____

_____

_____

_____

_____

_____

_____

HOW WILL I DEVELOP THEM?

_____

_____

_____

_____

_____

_____

_____

TOOLS/EQUIPMENT:

_____

_____

_____

_____

_____

_____

HOW WILL I GET THEM?

_____

_____

_____

_____

_____

_____

_____

DAY 18: PLAN YOUR IDEAL ROUTINE

Concept: A well-structured routine helps you stay consistent.

Activity: Design your ideal daily routine, reserving time for goals and habits.

MY IDEAL MORNING ROUTINE:

5:00 AM:

_____

6:00 AM:

_____

7:00 AM:

_____

8:00 AM:

_____

9:00 AM:

_____

MY WORK/DAY ROUTINE:

10:00 AM:
_____

12:00 PM:
_____

2:00 PM:
_____

4:00 PM:
_____

6:00 PM:
_____

MY IDEAL EVENING ROUTINE:

7:00 PM:

_____

8:00 PM:

_____

9:00 PM:

_____

10:00 PM:

_____

WHAT ADJUSTMENTS DO I NEED TO MAKE TO MY CURRENT ROUTINE?

_____

_____

_____

_____

_____

_____

_____

DAY 19: ESTABLISH YOUR REWARD SYSTEM

Concept: Rewards maintain motivation and celebrate achievements.

Activity: Define rewards for different levels of achievement.

REWARDS FOR DAILY ACHIEVEMENTS (HABITS COMPLETED):

_____

_____

_____

_____

_____

_____

REWARDS FOR WEEKLY ACHIEVEMENTS (WEEKLY GOALS MET):

_____

_____

_____

_____

_____

_____

REWARDS FOR MONTHLY ACHIEVEMENTS (MONTHLY GOALS MET):

_____

_____

_____

_____

_____

_____

REWARDS FOR IMPORTANT MILESTONES (SIGNIFICANT ACHIEVEMENTS):

_____

_____

_____

_____

_____

_____

HOW WILL I CELEBRATE WHEN I REACH MY MAIN GOAL?

_____

_____

_____

_____

_____

_____

_____

DAY 20: CREATE YOUR CONTINGENCY PLAN

Concept: There will always be difficult days. A backup plan maintains momentum.

Activity: Design "minimum" versions of your habits for complicated days.

THE PARACHUTE OF PROGRESS

WHEN I HAVE LITTLE TIME, MY MINIMUM VERSION IS:

Main habit: Normal:

_____

Minimum:

_____

Secondary habit: Normal:

_____

Minimum:

_____

WHEN I FEEL UNMOTIVATED, I WILL:

_____

_____

_____

_____

_____

_____

WHEN I FACE A CRISIS OR EMERGENCY, MY PRIORITY WILL BE:

_____

_____

_____

_____

_____

_____

_____

WHO CAN I TURN TO WHEN I NEED SUPPORT?

_____

_____

_____

_____

_____

_____

PERSONAL MOTIVATION PHRASES FOR DIFFICULT DAYS:

_____

_____

_____

_____

_____

_____

_____

PHASE 3: CULTIVATING WELLBEING AND AWARENESS

(DAYS 21-30)

DAY 21: SEEK SUPPORT AND ENCOURAGEMENT

Concept: It's easier to stay motivated when surrounded by positive people.

Activity: Identify 1-2 people who support you. Share a goal. Look for a like-minded community.

MY SUPPORT PEOPLE:

PERSON 1: _____

HOW CAN THEY HELP ME?

_____

_____

_____

_____

_____

WHAT GOAL DID I SHARE WITH THIS PERSON?

_____

_____

_____

_____

_____

_____

PERSON 2:

_____

_____

_____

_____

_____

_____

_____

HOW CAN THEY HELP ME?

_____

_____

_____

_____

_____

_____

_____

WHAT GOAL DID I SHARE WITH THIS PERSON?

_____

_____

_____

_____

_____

_____

COMMUNITIES OR GROUPS THAT COULD SUPPORT ME:

_____

_____

_____

_____

_____

_____

HOW CAN I SUPPORT OTHERS AS WELL?

_____

_____

_____

_____

_____

_____

_____

DAY 22: EMBRACE CHANGE

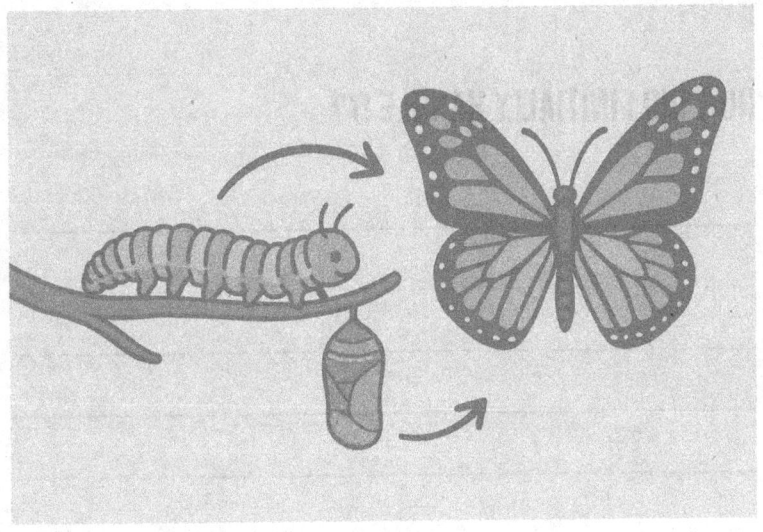

Concept: Change is vital for happiness and success. Accepting it allows you to grow.

Activity: Reflect on a recent change. How did you handle it? What did you learn? How will you embrace future changes with a growth mindset?

A RECENT CHANGE IN MY LIFE:

_____

_____

_____

_____

_____

HOW DID I INITIALLY HANDLE IT?

_____

_____

_____

_____

_____

_____

_____

WHAT DID I LEARN FROM THIS EXPERIENCE?

_____

_____

_____

_____

_____

_____

_____

WHAT WOULD I HAVE DONE DIFFERENTLY?

_____

_____

_____

_____

_____

_____

_____

HOW CAN I BETTER EMBRACE FUTURE CHANGES?

1.

2.

3.

MY NEW MINDSET TOWARD CHANGE:

_____

_____

_____

_____

_____

DAY 23: LET GO OF THE UNCONTROLLABLE

Concept: Trying to control everything can lead to frustration. You can control your reaction.

Activity: List 2-3 things that stress you and you can't control. Reframe your focus.

THINGS THAT STRESS ME AND I CAN'T CONTROL:

_____

_____

_____

_____

_____

_____

_____

HOW CAN I CHANGE MY ATTITUDE TOWARD THIS?

_____

_____

_____

_____

_____

_____

_____

WHAT CAN I FOCUS ON?

_____

_____

_____

_____

_____

_____

_____

HOW CAN I CHANGE MY ATTITUDE TOWARD THIS?

_____

_____

_____

_____

_____

_____

_____

WHAT CAN I FOCUS ON?

_____

_____

_____

_____

_____

_____

_____

HOW CAN I CHANGE MY ATTITUDE TOWARD THIS?

_____

_____

_____

_____

_____

_____

WHAT CAN I FOCUS ON?

_____

_____

_____

_____

_____

_____

_____

MY NEW PHILOSOPHY OF CONTROL:

_____

_____

_____

_____

_____

_____

DAY 24: CULTIVATE POSITIVE SELF-TALK

Concept: A poorly managed mind can be destructive. Replace negative thoughts with helpful affirmations.

Activity: Observe your self-talk. When a negative thought appears, challenge it and rewrite it.

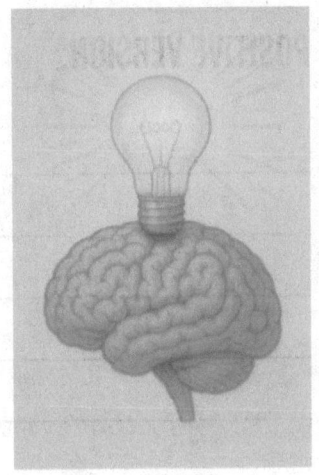

EXAMPLES:

NEGATIVE THOUGHT:

_____

_____

_____

_____

_____

POSITIVE VERSION:

_____

_____

_____

_____

_____

_____

_____

NEGATIVE THOUGHT:

_____

_____

_____

_____

_____

_____

_____

POSITIVE VERSION:

_____

_____

_____

_____

_____

_____

_____

NEGATIVE THOUGHT:

_____

_____

_____

_____

_____

_____

_____

POSITIVE VERSION:

_____

_____

_____

_____

_____

_____

_____

MY DAILY AFFIRMATIONS:

_____

_____

_____

_____

_____

_____

_____

WHEN AND HOW WILL I PRACTICE THESE AFFIRMATIONS?

_____

_____

_____

_____

_____

_____

DAY 25: ABANDON PROCRASTINATION, GUILT, AND EXCUSES

Concept: Procrastinating complicates everything; blaming denies responsibility; excuses stop progress.

Activity: Choose a postponed task. Take a small step today. Reflect on a situation where you blamed someone.

A TASK I'VE BEEN POSTPONING:

_____

_____

_____

_____

_____

_____

_____

WHY DID I AVOID IT?

_____

_____

_____

_____

_____

_____

_____

WHAT SMALL STEP CAN I TAKE TODAY?

_____

_____

_____

_____

_____

_____

WHAT STEP DID I TAKE TODAY?

_____

_____

_____

_____

_____

_____

A RECENT SITUATION WHERE I BLAMED SOMEONE:

_____

_____

_____

_____

_____

_____

_____

HOW DO I TAKE RESPONSIBILITY?

_____

_____

_____

_____

_____

_____

_____

MY COMMON EXCUSES AND HOW TO ELIMINATE THEM:

EXCUSE 1:

_____

_____

_____

_____

_____

INSTEAD I WILL SAY/DO:

_____

_____

_____

_____

_____

_____

EXCUSE 2:

_____

_____

_____

_____

_____

_____

_____

INSTEAD I WILL SAY/DO:

_____

_____

_____

_____

_____

_____

EXCUSE 3:

_____

_____

_____

_____

_____

_____

_____

INSTEAD I WILL SAY/DO:

_____

_____

_____

_____

_____

_____

DAY 26: FACE YOUR PROBLEMS AND FEARS

Concept: Fears and problems prevent decisions. Confronting them head-on is the best way.

Activity: Identify an avoided fear or problem. Write 2-3 incremental steps to face it.

AN AVOIDED FEAR OR PROBLEM:

_____

_____

_____

_____

_____

_____

WHY DOES IT SCARE ME?

_____

_____

_____

_____

_____

_____

_____

WHAT WOULD BE THE WORST POSSIBLE SCENARIO?

_____

_____

_____

_____

_____

_____

_____

Real probability of that scenario: _____%

BENEFITS OF FACING IT:

_____

_____

_____

_____

_____

_____

_____

Action plan:

STEP 1 (SMALL):

_____

_____

_____

_____

_____

Deadline: _____

STEP 2 (MEDIUM):

_____

_____

_____

_____

Deadline: _____

STEP 3 (COMPLETE):

_____

_____

_____

_____

_____

Deadline: _____

WHO CAN SUPPORT ME?

_____

_____

_____

_____

_____

_____

DAY 27: DEVELOP EMOTIONAL INTELLIGENCE

THE EMOTIONAL COMPASS

Concept: Recognizing, understanding, and managing your own emotions, as well as those of others, is key.

Activity: Reflect on your emotional patterns and define strategies.

MOST FREQUENT EMOTIONS:

POSITIVE:

_____

_____

_____

_____

_____

NEGATIVE:

_____

_____

_____

_____

_____

_____

_____

SITUATIONS THAT PROVOKE STRONG EMOTIONS:

SITUATION 1:

_____

_____

_____

_____

_____

EMOTION IT PROVOKES:

_____

_____

_____

_____

_____

_____

HOW TO HANDLE IT BETTER?

_____

_____

_____

_____

_____

_____

_____

SITUATION 2:

_____

_____

_____

_____

_____

_____

_____

EMOTION IT PROVOKES:

_____

_____

_____

_____

_____

_____

_____

HOW TO HANDLE IT BETTER?

_____

_____

_____

_____

_____

_____

_____

STRATEGIES FOR MANAGING DIFFICULT EMOTIONS:

_____

_____

_____

_____

_____

_____

HOW CAN I BE MORE EMPATHETIC WITH OTHERS?

_____

_____

_____

_____

_____

DAY 28: PRACTICE GRATITUDE AND MINDFULNESS

Concept: Gratitude focuses on the positive; mindfulness anchors you to the present.

Activity: Define a daily gratitude and mindfulness practice.

THE FLOWER OF
MINDFULNESS

CALM   BALANCE

THREE THINGS I'M GRATEFUL FOR TODAY:

Why am I grateful for each one?

#1:

_____

_____

_____

_____

#2:

_____

_____

_____

_____

_____

_____

#3:

_____

_____

_____

_____

_____

_____

_____

MY PRACTICE WILL BE:

☐ Meditation (_____ minutes daily)

☐ Conscious breathing

☐ Mindful walks

☐ Mindful eating

☐ Other:

_____

_____

_____

_____

_____

_____

_____

WHEN WILL I PRACTICE IT EACH DAY?

_____

_____

_____

_____

HOW DO I FEEL WHEN I PRACTICE GRATITUDE AND MINDFULNESS?

_____

_____

_____

_____

_____

DAY 29: BUILD AND STRENGTHEN RELATIONSHIPS

Concept: Strong relationships predict happiness and well-being.

Activity: Contact someone important. Express gratitude.

IMPORTANT PEOPLE IN MY LIFE:

FAMILY:

_____

_____

_____

_____

_____

_____

FRIENDS:

_____

_____

_____

_____

_____

COLLEAGUES/MENTORS:

_____

_____

_____

_____

_____

_____

_____

WHO DID I CONTACT TODAY?

_____

_____

_____

_____

_____

_____

WHAT DID I SAY/WRITE TO THEM?

_____

_____

_____

_____

_____

_____

_____

WHO DID I EXPRESS GRATITUDE TO TODAY?

_____

_____

_____

_____

_____

_____

_____

HOW DID I DO IT?

_____

_____

_____

_____

_____

_____

_____

HOW CAN I BE MORE INTENTIONAL IN MY RELATIONSHIPS?

1.

2.

3.

DAY 30: SIMPLIFY AND ORGANIZE YOUR LIFE

Concept: Physical and mental clutter consumes energy. Simplifying brings clarity.

Activity: Organize a space and eliminate commitments that don't add value.

AREA I ORGANIZED TODAY:

_____

_____

_____

_____

_____

_____

WHAT DID I ELIMINATE/DONATE/ORGANIZE?

_____

_____

_____

_____

_____

_____

HOW DO I FEEL IN THIS SPACE NOW?

_____

_____

_____

_____

_____

_____

_____

COMMITMENTS I CAN ELIMINATE:

_____

_____

_____

_____

_____

_____

_____

WHY CAN I ELIMINATE THEM?

_____

_____

_____

_____

_____

_____

_____

MY NEW PHILOSOPHY ON SIMPLICITY:

_____

_____

_____

_____

_____

_____

_____

PHASE 4: DEEPENING YOUR BEST LIFE AND CONTINUOUS GROWTH

(DAYS 31-40)

DAY 31: PHYSICAL WELLBEING – SLEEP AND EXERCISE

Concept: Getting enough sleep and exercising improves your overall health.

Activity: Sleep an extra hour today. Walk for 30 minutes or engage in a physical activity you enjoy.

MY CURRENT SLEEP ROUTINE:

What time do I normally go to bed?

_____

What time do I normally wake up?

_____

How many hours do I sleep on average?

_____

QUALITY OF MY SLEEP:

- ☐ Excellent
- ☐ Good
- ☐ Fair
- ☐ Poor

TO IMPROVE MY SLEEP, I WILL:

_____

_____

_____

_____

_____

PHYSICAL ACTIVITY TODAY:

_____

_____

_____

_____

_____

Duration: _____

HOW DO I FEEL AFTER EXERCISE?

_____

_____

_____

_____

_____

_____

HOW DID I FEEL PRIORITIZING SLEEP AND EXERCISE TODAY?

_____

_____

_____

_____

_____

_____

DAY 32: PHYSICAL WELLBEING – NUTRITION AND HYDRATION

Concept: Reduce sugar and caffeine. Drink enough water.

Activity: Eliminate one sugary food today. Replace one beverage with water.

MY TYPICAL DIET:

BREAKFAST:

_____

_____

_____

_____

_____

_____

LUNCH:

_____

_____

_____

_____

_____

DINNER:

_____

_____

_____

_____

_____

_____

_____

FREQUENT SNACKS:

_____

_____

_____

_____

_____

_____

_____

SUGAR ELIMINATED TODAY:

_____

_____

_____

_____

_____

_____

_____

WHY DID I CHOOSE IT?

_____

_____

_____

_____

_____

_____

_____

BEVERAGE REPLACED WITH WATER:

_____

_____

_____

_____

_____

GLASSES OF WATER TODAY: _____

HOW DO I FEEL WITH THESE CHANGES?

_____

_____

_____

_____

_____

NUTRITION AND HYDRATION NOTES:

_____

_____

_____

_____

_____

_____

PERMANENT CHANGES I WILL MAKE:

1.

2.

3.

DAY 33: MENTAL WELLBEING – READ AND EXERCISE YOUR BRAIN

Concept: Reading inspires; exercising the mind prepares you to solve problems.

Activity: Read an inspiring book. Do a mentally demanding activity.

BOOKS ON MY LIST:

_____

_____

_____

_____

_____

_____

_____

CURRENT INSPIRING BOOK:

_____

_____

_____

_____

_____

_____

_____

WHAT IS IT ABOUT?

_____

_____

_____

_____

_____

_____

_____

WHAT DID I READ TODAY?

_____

_____

_____

_____

_____

_____

IDEA OR CONCEPT THAT IMPACTED ME MOST:

_____

_____

_____

_____

_____

_____

_____

MENTAL ACTIVITY TODAY:

- ☐ Puzzles/Sudoku
- ☐ Crosswords
- ☐ Chess
- ☐ Learning something new
- ☐ Solving a complex problem
- ☐ Other:

_____

Duration: _____

WHAT DID I LEARN OR PRACTICE?

_____

_____

_____

_____

_____

_____

_____

HOW CAN I MAKE LEARNING A DAILY HABIT?

_____

_____

_____

_____

_____

DAY 34: EMOTIONAL WELLBEING – LAUGH AND HELP

Concept: Laughter and service enhance your overall well-being.

Activity: Look for opportunities to laugh. Help someone, even with a small gesture.

WHAT MADE ME LAUGH TODAY?

SITUATION 1:

_____

_____

_____

_____

_____

SITUATION 2:

_____

_____

_____

_____

_____

_____

_____

WHO DID I SHARE LAUGHTER WITH?

_____

_____

_____

_____

_____

_____

HOW DID I FEEL AFTERWARD?

_____

_____

_____

_____

_____

_____

HOW DID I HELP SOMEONE TODAY?

_____

_____

_____

_____

_____

_____

_____

WHO DID I HELP?

_____

_____

_____

_____

_____

_____

HOW DID THEY REACT?

_____

_____

_____

_____

_____

_____

_____

HOW DID HELPING MAKE ME FEEL?

_____

_____

_____

_____

_____

_____

_____

WAYS TO HELP REGULARLY:

1.

2.

3.

SOURCES OF JOY AND HUMOR IN MY LIFE:

_____

_____

_____

_____

_____

DAY 35: DISCONNECT FROM DEVICES AND COMPARISONS

Concept: Disconnecting before sleep improves rest. Avoiding comparisons on social media improves self-esteem.

Activity: Establish a screen-free schedule.

CURRENT DEVICE USAGE:

Hours per day on phone: _____

MOST USED APPS:

_____

_____

_____

_____

_____

Daily time on social media: _____

DIGITAL DISCONNECTION PLAN:

Screen-free schedule: from _____ to _____

WHAT WILL I DO INSTEAD OF USING DEVICES?

_____

_____

_____

_____

_____

_____

_____

HOW DO I FEEL WHEN I'M NOT CONSTANTLY CONNECTED TO MY PHONE?

_____

_____

_____

_____

_____

REFLECTIONS ON COMPARING MYSELF TO OTHERS:

WHO DO I FREQUENTLY COMPARE MYSELF TO?

_____

_____

_____

_____

_____

_____

_____

HOW DOES IT MAKE ME FEEL?

_____

_____

_____

_____

_____

_____

_____

WHAT IS REAL AND WHAT IS "THE BEST" ON SOCIAL MEDIA?

_____

_____

_____

_____

_____

_____

_____

MY REFLECTIONS ON DIGITAL DISCONNECTION:

_____

_____

_____

_____

_____

_____

_____

PERMANENT CHANGES IN MY TECHNOLOGY USE:

1.

2.

3.

DAY 36: ANNUAL REFLECTION AND LESSONS LEARNED

Concept: Review goals and learnings each year.

Activity: Open the "Annual Reflections" section. Record achievements and lessons.

ANNUAL REFLECTIONS.

Year: _____

GREATEST ACHIEVEMENTS:

_____

_____

_____

_____

_____

_____

GREATEST CHALLENGES:

_____

_____

_____

_____

_____

_____

HOW DID I GROW THIS YEAR?

_____

_____

_____

_____

_____

MOST IMPORTANT LESSONS:

LESSON 1:

_____

_____

_____

_____

_____

_____

_____

LESSON 2:

_____

_____

_____

_____

_____

_____

LESSON 3:

_____

_____

_____

_____

_____

_____

GOALS ACHIEVED THIS YEAR:

_____

_____

_____

_____

_____

_____

_____

GOALS NOT ACHIEVED AND WHY:

_____

_____

_____

_____

_____

_____

_____

WHAT WILL I DO DIFFERENTLY NEXT YEAR?

_____

_____

_____

_____

_____

_____

KEYWORD FOR NEXT YEAR:

_____

_____

_____

_____

_____

_____

DAY 37: FLEXIBILITY AND GOAL ADAPTATION

Concept: Goals change over time. If a goal no longer attracts you, let it go or adjust it.

Activity: Review a long-term goal and update it if necessary.

GOAL 1:

_____

_____

_____

_____

_____

_____

_____

IS IT STILL RELEVANT?

- ☐ Yes
- ☐ No
- ☐ Partially

WHY?

_____

_____

_____

_____

_____

HOW WILL I ADJUST IT?

_____

_____

_____

_____

_____

GOAL 2:

_____

_____

_____

_____

_____

_____

IS IT STILL RELEVANT?

- ☐ Yes
- ☐ No
- ☐ Partially

WHY?

_____

_____

_____

_____

_____

HOW WILL I ADJUST IT?

_____

_____

_____

_____

_____

_____

_____

GOAL 3:

_____

_____

_____

_____

_____

_____

IS IT STILL RELEVANT?

- ☐ Yes
- ☐ No
- ☐ Partially

WHY?

_____

_____

_____

_____

_____

HOW WILL I ADJUST IT?

_____

_____

_____

_____

_____

_____

HOW HAVE I ADAPTED MY PLANS BASED ON MY EXPERIENCE?

_____

_____

_____

_____

_____

_____

NEW GOAL I WANT TO ADD:

_____

_____

_____

_____

_____

WHY IS IT IMPORTANT NOW?

_____

_____

_____

_____

_____

DAY 38: MAINTAIN THE VISION OF BEING A BETTER PERSON

Concept: Ask yourself: "Am I giving my life the best I have to offer?"

Activity: Choose one aspect of your life and define concrete actions.

AM I GIVING MY LIFE THE BEST I HAVE TO OFFER?

- ☐ Definitely yes
- ☐ In most areas
- ☐ In some areas
- ☐ Need to improve a lot

ASPECT I CHOSE TO IMPROVE:

_____

_____

_____

_____

_____

_____

_____

HOW WILL I GIVE IT MY BEST?

_____

_____

_____

_____

_____

_____

CONCRETE ACTIONS:

ACTION 1:

_____

_____

_____

_____

_____

Start date: _____

ACTION 2:

_____

_____

_____

_____

_____

Start date: _____

ACTION 3:

_____

_____

_____

_____

_____

_____

_____

Start date: _____

WHAT INSPIRES ME TO BE A BETTER PERSON?

_____

_____

_____

_____

_____

_____

MY DEFINITION OF "BEING A BETTER PERSON":

_____

_____

_____

_____

_____

_____

MY COMMITMENT:

_____

_____

_____

_____

_____

_____

DAY 39: MASTERY OF THE DAY — TURN GOALS INTO HABITS

Concept: Achievement is built with daily actions.

Activity: Choose a pending goal. Reduce it to the smallest possible habit. Start tomorrow.

MY MOST IMPORTANT PENDING GOAL:

_____

_____

_____

_____

_____

_____

WHY IS IT IMPORTANT?

_____

_____

_____

_____

_____

_____

SMALLEST DAILY HABIT THAT BRINGS ME CLOSER TO THE GOAL:

_____

_____

_____

_____

_____

_____

Daily habit duration: _____

WHEN WILL I DO IT EACH DAY?

_____

_____

_____

_____

_____

_____

WHAT DO I NEED TO MAKE IT POSSIBLE?

_____

_____

_____

_____

_____

_____

CONTINGENCY PLAN IF I CAN'T DO IT ONE DAY:

_____

_____

_____

_____

_____

_____

My commitment: I commit to this habit for _____ consecutive days, starting tomorrow.

REWARDS FOR MAINTAINING THE HABIT:

_____

_____

_____

_____

_____

AFTER 7 DAYS:

_____

_____

_____

_____

_____

AFTER 30 DAYS:

_____

_____

_____

_____

_____

_____

AFTER 90 DAYS:

_____

_____

_____

_____

_____

_____

_____

GOAL AND "SMALLEST HABIT" (SUMMARY):

_____

_____

_____

_____

_____

_____

_____

DAY 40: CELEBRATION AND ONGOING COMMITMENT

Concept: When you achieve a goal, celebrate. Your manual is a work in progress.

Activity: Celebrate your 40-day progress. Review your manual. Write your commitment to continue.

CELEBRATION OF MY 40 DAYS

WHAT DID I ACCOMPLISH?

_____

_____

_____

_____

_____

HOW DO I FEEL DIFFERENT COMPARED TO DAY 1?

_____

_____

_____

_____

_____

_____

MY GREATEST INSIGHTS:

INSIGHT 1:

_____

_____

_____

_____

_____

INSIGHT 2:

_____

_____

_____

_____

_____

_____

INSIGHT 3:

_____

_____

_____

_____

_____

_____

_____

HABITS I DEVELOPED:

_____

_____

_____

_____

_____

_____

_____

HOW WILL I CELEBRATE THIS ACHIEVEMENT?

_____

_____

_____

_____

_____

_____

_____

MY PERSONAL COMMITMENT:

_____

_____

_____

_____

_____

_____

_____

Date: _____

Signature: _____

FINAL REFLECTION AND CLOSING

REVIEW YOUR 40 DAYS

WHAT CHANGED IN YOUR CLARITY?

_____

_____

_____

_____

_____

_____

_____

WHAT CHANGED IN YOUR PURPOSE?

_____

_____

_____

_____

_____

_____

_____

WHAT CHANGED IN YOUR PERSONAL GROWTH?

_____

_____

_____

_____

_____

_____

_____

THREE MOST SIGNIFICANT CHANGES IN MY LIFE:

1.

2.

3.

HOW WILL I CONTINUE USING THIS MANUAL?

☐ I will review it weekly

☐ I will review it monthly

☐ I will review it quarterly

☐ I will create a version 2.0

☐ Other:

_____

MY PLAN TO MAINTAIN MOMENTUM:

_____

_____

_____

_____

_____

_____

_____

CONGRATULATIONS!

You have successfully completed your 40-day journey toward a clearer, more intentional, and fulfilling life.

THE GOAL ACHIEVED

This is not the end, but the beginning of a life lived with purpose. You have built the foundations of your personal life manual, a tool that will accompany you and evolve with you.

REMEMBER:

- Your life manual is a living document — update it regularly.
- Personal growth is a journey, not a destination — be patient with yourself.
- Consistent small steps create incredible transformations — maintain your daily habits.
- Celebrate your achievements — both big and small.
- Share your light with others — your growth inspires those around you.

Your next stage: continue living with clarity and purpose. Return to this manual when you need guidance or motivation. The life you dream of is within reach of your daily decisions.

ADDITIONAL RESOURCES FOR YOUR CONTINUOUS GROWTH

MONTHLY REVIEW TEMPLATE

Month: _____ Year: _____

WHAT DID I ACCOMPLISH THIS MONTH?

_____

_____

_____

_____

_____

WHAT CHALLENGES DID I FACE?

_____

_____

_____

_____

_____

_____

_____

WHAT DID I LEARN?

_____

_____

_____

_____

_____

_____

_____

WHAT ADJUSTMENTS WILL I MAKE NEXT MONTH?

_____

_____

_____

_____

_____

ANNUAL REVIEW TEMPLATE

HOW DID I GROW THIS YEAR?

_____

_____

_____

_____

_____

WHAT GOALS DID I ACHIEVE/NOT ACHIEVE?

_____

_____

_____

_____

_____

_____

WHAT CHANGES WILL I MAKE TO MY MANUAL?

_____

_____

_____

_____

_____

_____

PERSONAL NOTES

_____

_____

_____

_____

_____

_____

_____

ABOUT THE AUTHOR

Claudio Alvarez is an educa-
tor, motivator, and passionate
advocate for personal growth
and self-discovery. With over
several decades of experience
guiding young people in
educational and personal
development settings, he has
dedicated his life to helping
others align their daily actions
with their higher purpose.

Through his work as a teacher and mentor, Claudio
inspires students and adults alike to reflect deeply, act
intentionally, and build lives rooted in clarity, respect,
and self-discipline. His approach combines motivation,
mindfulness, and practical strategies for success—
empowering each person to grow academically, emotion-
ally, and spiritually.

Claudio believes that true transformation begins within —through awareness, reflection, and consistent daily action. This manual embodies his vision: to provide tools and guidance that help others design lives filled with meaning, purpose, and joy.

His message is simple and powerful: *You have the power to create your best life—one step at a time.*